COMBATING RELIGIOUS DISCRIMINATION TODAY: FINAL REPORT

U.S. Department of Justice

July 2016

Justice.Gov/Combating_Religious_Discrimination

Dear Colleagues and Community Leaders:

One of our nation's fundamental principles is that all people – regardless of where they worship or what they believe – are entitled to equal protection and fair treatment under the law. This longstanding embrace of religious pluralism and respect for diversity has made our country a beacon of hope and a place of refuge for people from all across the globe.

Sadly, we have not always lived up to these lofty ideals. And even today, far too many people in this country face discrimination, harassment, and violence simply because of their religious beliefs. The Federal government is committed to eradicating the scourge of discrimination and bigotry in all of its forms. That is why in December 2015, I was privileged to announce that the Department of Justice's Civil Rights Division, in collaboration with our outstanding U.S. Attorney and Federal agency partners, would be launching "Combating Religious Discrimination Today," a community engagement initiative designed to promote religious freedom, challenge religious discrimination, and enhance our efforts to combat religion-based hate violence and crimes. Over the last several months, I have joined my colleagues from across the Federal government as we traveled around the country, engaging in a series of roundtables with diverse religious leaders, civil rights organizations, and community members. We used these discussions to hear from a wide range of stakeholders, so we can better understand the barriers of religious discrimination and the challenges to religious freedom they face in their communities. We also solicited their specific recommendations about how the Federal government can best address these barriers and challenges. The roundtables produced a rich, productive, and informative dialogue about some of the defining civil rights issues of our time.

I want to acknowledge and thank the many religious leaders and community partners who gave their valuable time to participate in this initiative, often traveling great distances, and who shared their ideas and experiences with great thoughtfulness and introspection. I especially thank those Roundtable Participants who prepared and submitted information that helped focus the discussion and volunteered to guide the conversation during the roundtables. Your contributions were invaluable in allowing us to gain a deeper understanding about the challenges we face and the solutions we need to fulfill our country's founding ideals of inclusivity, equality, and opportunity for all. I also want to recognize my colleagues across the Federal government who invested so much time and energy into this project, especially the Departments of Education, Labor, and Homeland Security; the Equal Employment Opportunity Commission; and within the Department of Justice, the Federal Bureau of Investigation, the Community Relations Service, and the U.S. Attorneys' Offices. In addition, I want to thank the White House, and particularly the Office of Faith-based and Neighborhood Partnerships and the Initiative on Asian Americans and Pacific Islanders, for their assistance and leadership in this effort. Your partnership in this and so many other efforts is vital in our work to protect the civil rights of all who live in America.

This entire initiative has been premised on the notion that we in the Federal government need to ensure we are hearing from impacted communities. And to that end, this report is not focused on representing the views of the Department of Justice or any of the other agencies that participated in the roundtables. Rather, it provides an overview of what we heard and learned at the roundtables, detailing the challenges identified, themes highlighted, and recommendations proposed. As you will see, on some topics we heard wide agreement. On others we heard a range of different perspectives. Either way, we tried to capture the essence and key points from the Participants about the issues facing their communities.

We hope that memorializing these ideas and recommendations will facilitate consideration and implementation of action items on the part of the Federal government and non-governmental organizations. We also hope to continue to encourage meaningful dialogue among diverse communities, religious groups, and the Federal government. Through dialogue, collaboration, and conversation lies our greatest ability to better understand the differences among us and to create the safe, inclusive, and vibrant communities that we all aspire to build.

I hope you find this report useful and informative as we work together in our shared mission to better understand the differences among us, as well as the common hopes, aspirations, and concerns we share.

Sincerely,

Vanita Gupta

Principal Deputy Assistant Attorney General
Civil Rights Division, U.S. Department of Justice

Dear Colleagues:

As President Obama has said, "From many faiths and diverse beliefs, Americans are united by the ideals we cherish. Our shared values define who we are as a people and what we stand for as a Nation." This Administration celebrates the commitment of the United States to religious freedom, non-discrimination, and religious pluralism, and is dedicated to upholding those principles and values.

As part of that work, we invited governmental and civil society leaders to the White House in December 2015 to discuss opportunities and challenges in this area. At that time, U.S. Department of Justice Civil Rights Division's Principal Deputy Assistant Attorney General, Vanita Gupta, announced that roundtables would be held across the country to explore the state of religious freedom and gather recommendations about how the Federal government can address these issues.

This report memorializes those discussions, and it is an honor to be able to release it at another White House gathering today. We want to thank all of the religious and community leaders who contributed to the report. We also want to thank the Department of Justice's Civil Rights Division for its leadership of this project as well as the U.S. Attorneys and Federal agency partners who contributed.

President Obama said during his recent visit to a Baltimore mosque:

> If we're serious about freedom of religion . . . we have to understand an attack on one faith is an attack on all our faiths. And when any religious group is targeted, we all have a responsibility to speak up. And we have to reject a politics that seeks to manipulate prejudice or bias, and targets people because of religion.

> [N]one of us can be silent. We can't be bystanders to bigotry. And together, we've got to show that America truly protects all faiths.

In collaboration with the dedicated religious and other civil society leaders as well as our governmental partners, we look forward to continuing to show that America truly protects all faiths.

Sincerely,

Melissa Rogers

Melissa Rogers

Special Assistant to the President and Executive Director
White House Office of Faith-based and Neighborhood Partnerships

TABLE OF CONTENTS

I. Introduction

A. Our Nation's History of Religious Pluralism and Diversity

For centuries, America has stood throughout the world as a beacon of religious diversity and pluralism. People of many faiths, creeds, and backgrounds have arrived on our shores in search of protection, freedom, and opportunity. The framers of the Constitution ensured that there shall be no religious test for public office, and they placed religious freedom as the first right listed in the First Amendment of the Bill of Rights, with its dual protections ensuring that the government shall not take sides in religious matters, and that free religious exercise would be protected. The centrality of these beliefs to the foundation of this country can be seen in the Virginia Statute on Religious Freedom, which was drafted by Thomas Jefferson and served as the precursor for the First Amendment's Establishment and Free Exercise Clauses. Enacted in 1786, it provided that "no man shall be compelled to frequent or support any religious worship, place, or ministry," nor "suffer on account of his religious opinions or belief." As President Obama has remarked: "The Virginia Statute was more than a law. It was a statement of principle, declaring freedom of religion as the natural right of all humanity – not a privilege for any government to give or take away."

The United States has long been religiously diverse – from the multiplicity of Christian sects and other faiths in its early days, to an incredibly rich diversity of faiths today. Throughout our history, religious dissenters and minorities have found protection in our laws and institutions, from Quaker conscientious objectors during the Civil War to Jehovah's Witnesses refusing to recite the pledge of allegiance in school during World War II, among many others. However, as with other foundational rights, our country has not always lived up to the promise of religious freedom and equal treatment for all. Roman Catholics and Mormons in the 19th century, Jews in the 19th and 20th centuries, and many others have experienced discrimination – and even at times persecution – throughout our history. In light of this, Congress has enacted a number of laws that prohibit religion-based discrimination. For example, several provisions of the landmark Civil Rights Act of 1964 contain explicit protections for religion, including Title II (public accommodations), Title III (public facilities), Title IV (education), and Title VII (employment). Likewise, the Fair Housing Act of 1968 forbids discrimination based on religion. More recent statutes include the Religious Land Use and Institutionalized Persons Act, which prohibits local governments from adopting or enforcing land use regulations that discriminate against religious assemblies and institutions, or which unjustifiably burden religious exercise. This law also protects the religious exercise of persons confined to certain institutions. There are also a number of Federal statutes that criminalize acts of violence based on religion or directed towards houses of worship, including the Matthew Shepard and James Byrd, Jr. Hate Crimes Prevention Act of 2009.[1] These federal laws have been, and continue to be, enforced by a range of Federal agencies.

B. Current Challenges to Religious Diversity in America

Today, here in the 21st century, our country is more religiously diverse than ever before. A recent survey from the Pew Research Center reported that roughly 70.6 percent of the country's population identifies as Christian; 22.8 percent as unaffiliated with a religion; 1.9 percent as Jewish; 0.9 percent as Muslim; 0.7 percent as Buddhist; 0.7 percent as Hindu; 1.5 percent as observant of other

---

[1] For more information about these laws, please refer to Appendix A.

faiths; and 0.3 percent as observant of another world religion. Given current demographic trends, it is likely that our nation will only continue to become increasingly diverse in the upcoming years.

This rich pluralism, while a source of pride and inspiration, also brings its own set of challenges. A constant theme throughout our discussions in this initiative was that members of less familiar or populous religious communities recounted being regularly confronted by misperceptions and false stereotypes about their faith traditions. Many communities noted that the lack of understanding about the diversity of religious practice in this country often leads to discrimination, harassment, and violence. There was widespread agreement that there is a need for the public to gain greater knowledge about these faith traditions and also to recognize that belief systems that may seem less familiar within the context of the historical American religious experience deserve respect and equal treatment. There was also discussion about how the growing diversity of values and beliefs – which includes the significant segment of the population that does not readily identify with any particular religious tradition or professes no faith – requires additional public discussion about how the term "religion" is defined and the ways in which these populations can experience discrimination and mistreatment.

Another theme that emerged during the initiative was the backlash of violence and harassment that Muslims, as well as individuals perceived to be Muslim, including Sikhs, Hindus, Arabs, Middle Easterners, and South Asians, continue to face. Since the attacks of September 11, 2001, this country has witnessed waves of unjustified discrimination and violence directed towards these communities. Following recent horrific terrorist attacks over the past year – both at home and abroad – such actions have only increased in intensity and frequency. Communities reported an uptick in attacks and threats against mosques, gurdwaras, and other houses of worship, as well as acts of bullying, harassment, and violence against children and adults who are – or are perceived to be – Muslim. We also heard repeatedly that these acts are deeply distressing not only because of the harm they inflict on the impacted individuals and communities, but also because discrimination that targets one religious or faith community harms us all. There was uniform consensus that such acts violate the defining values of our country and tear at the very core of what makes America such a strong, powerful, and free nation: the diversity of our people and our dedication to the core principles of liberty and equality.

Even beyond the experience of these particular communities, many others highlighted that despite the existence of a number of statutes that prohibit religious discrimination, there remain significant gaps between the protections of our laws and the experiences of people in their daily lives. Communities recounted how many people are confronted with discrimination and harassment and do not know where to turn for support or assistance. There was agreement that the Federal government needs to enhance its outreach, improve its communications, and streamline its bureaucracy. By making government more accessible and approachable, we can ensure that all people receive the full protections embedded in our laws. Particularly in an ever-evolving climate of new technology, today the Federal government has opportunities to engage with diverse communities through a variety of media, from more traditional forms of communication, to the use of the Internet and social media.

Finally, during this initiative we heard from a diverse array of community members that there are ongoing concerns about the ways in which some communities feel that their religious freedoms are being challenged or curtailed. There was also an acknowledgement that in regards to the Religious Freedom Restoration Act – which was enacted by Congress in 1993 as a measure to protect the rights of religious individuals and communities that may be burdened by government activity – further conversations may be needed to ensure the actions of the Federal government do not unnecessarily impede religious exercise and expression.

C. Overview of Combating Religious Discrimination Today

In December 2015, the White House hosted a convening entitled "Celebrating and Protecting America's Tradition of Religious Pluralism." That event highlighted our nation's rich religious diversity, but also acknowledged ongoing challenges that people of different religious faiths continue to face. During that convening, Vanita Gupta, head of the Justice Department's Civil Rights Division, announced that in the upcoming months the Justice Department would partner with other Federal agencies to host a series of community roundtable discussions, aiming to "better understand how the scourge of religious discrimination continues to undermine opportunity." A few months later, the Justice Department officially launched "Combating Religious Discrimination Today," an interagency community engagement initiative designed to promote religious freedom, challenge religious discrimination, and enhance enforcement of religion-based hate crimes.

From March to June 2016, the Civil Rights Division, in partnership with U.S. Attorneys and other Federal agencies, hosted seven community roundtables across the country that focused on protecting people and places of worship from religion-based hate crimes (Dallas, Texas); combating religious discrimination, including bullying, in education (Stanford, California and Newark, New Jersey) and employment (Birmingham, Alabama); and addressing unlawful barriers that interfere with the construction of places of worship (Detroit, Michigan). Each of these issue topics is not only a domain where Federal agencies have jurisdiction to address religion-based discrimination, but also represents an area where many religious leaders and community members have raised specific concerns in recent months. Additionally, the Civil Rights Division held two roundtables in Washington, D.C., which brought together national advocacy and religious organizations to review themes and proposals from the discussions in order to use what we learned to improve upon existing government resources and efforts in these areas.[2]

---

[2] For more information about the roundtables and the organizations that attended them, please refer to Appendix B.

Government officials and community members discussed issues related to religious discrimination in employment at a roundtable held in Birmingham, Alabama, on April 20, 2016.

Agencies that participated in the roundtables include the Departments of Education, Homeland Security (DHS), and Labor (DOL); the Equal Employment Opportunity Commission (EEOC); the White House Initiative on Asian Americans and Pacific Islanders; the White House Office of Faith-based and Neighborhood Partnerships; and within the Justice Department, the Civil Rights Division, Federal Bureau of Investigation (FBI), Office of Justice Programs, Executive Office for U.S. Attorneys, and Community Relations Service.

Roundtable Location	Date	Topic	Agency Co-Sponsors and Participants
Newark, NJ	March 8, 2016	Education	U.S. Attorney's Office for the District of New Jersey; White House Initiative on Asian Americans and Pacific Islanders; Department of Education; Community Relations Service; Civil Rights Division
Dallas, TX	March 29, 2016	Hate Crimes	U.S. Attorney's Office for the Northern District of Texas; U.S. Attorney's Office for the District of Kansas; Department of Homeland Security; Federal Bureau of Investigation; Community Relations Service; Civil Rights Division
Birmingham, AL	April 20, 2016	Employment	U.S. Attorney's Office for the Northern District of Alabama; Department of Labor; Equal Employment Opportunity Commission; Civil Rights Division
Detroit, MI	May 2, 2016	Religious Land Use	U.S. Attorney's Office for the Eastern District of Michigan; Community Relations Service; Civil Rights Division
Stanford, CA	May 16, 2016	Education	U.S. Attorney's Office for the Northern District of California; U.S. Attorney's Office for the Eastern District of California; U.S. Attorney's Office for the Southern District of California; U.S. Attorney's Office for the Central District of California; U.S. Attorney's Office for the District of Idaho; Department of Education; White House Initiative on Asian Americans and Pacific Islanders; Civil Rights Division
Washington, D.C.	May 26, 2016	National Issue Review	Department of Labor; Department of Education; Equal Employment Opportunity Commission; Federal Bureau of Investigation; White House Office of Faith-based and Neighborhood Partnerships; Civil Rights Division
Washington, D.C.	June 20, 2016	Defining Religion and Religious Discrimination	Department of Homeland Security; Department of Labor; Department of Education; Equal Employment Opportunity Commission; Civil Rights Division

In advance of each roundtable discussion, Federal government officials invited a diverse group of religious leaders, community members, civil rights advocates, academics, students, and others to share their views about common themes regarding religious discrimination and to propose specific recommendations that the Federal government can implement to more effectively address these issues. For each roundtable, Participants were invited to submit discussion topics that were used to shape the agenda. Following the discussions, we asked Participants to continue to share any additional suggestions and recommendations about how the Federal government can enhance and improve its efforts to combat religious discrimination, harassment, and violence across an array of areas. A full list of organizations and participants at each roundtable is detailed later in this report. They include representatives from a range of communities and perspectives, including, among others, Jewish, Christian, Muslim, Hindu, Sikh, South-Asian, Arab, and non-religious communities.

The roundtables yielded a rich discussion about the state of religious freedom, religious discrimination, and religion-based hate crimes in the United States. The roundtables also generated many proposals for actions that Participants believe the Federal government – and community groups working together – should implement to further the protection of the vital principles of religious pluralism, diversity, and freedom. We have sought throughout this report to capture faithfully the observations, ideas, and recommendations of the Participants. The inclusion of these in this report does not reflect – nor should it be read – as problems confirmed or recommendations supported by any of the Federal government participants.

II. Common Themes and Recommendations

A. Education

Federal laws, including Title IV of the Civil Rights Act of 1964 (Title IV), prohibit religious discrimination in educational institutions. Yet despite these protections, students of all ages and grade levels too often find themselves bullied or harassed because of their religious beliefs. Roundtable Participants, while recognizing limitations on teaching about religion or religious practices in schools, also regularly returned to the theme of making sure that our nation's students learn about – and develop an understanding of – diverse religious communities. Participants repeatedly emphasized the need for additional guidance, more robust outreach, and enhanced communication about Federal government resources around all of these issues.

Themes, Trends, and Problems:

Increase in Religion-Based Bullying and Harassment: Roundtable Participants reported a noticeable uptick in cases of bullying and harassment against religious communities and students. A number of Participants specifically highlighted an increase in bullying against Muslim, Sikh, Hindu, Arab, Middle Eastern, and South Asian students, as well as students perceived to be members of these communities. Participants attributed this rise to backlash stemming from recent terrorist attacks, as well as a result of an increase in anti-Muslim rhetoric in the United States. Participants also referenced studies about the impact of bullying on Sikh and Hindu communities. A number of Participants observed that other communities – including various Jewish and Christian communities – also remain at risk of religion-based bullying and harassment. Bullying and harassment of nonreligious students and religion-based discrimination against lesbian, gay, bisexual, or transgender students were also identified as concerns by Participants. While recognizing these serious and growing concerns about religion-based bullying and harassment, some Participants also emphasized the need to distinguish between unlawful conduct and the expression of less "popular" or less "traditional" religious viewpoints. Roundtable Participants also applauded the Department of Education's decision to require school districts to report allegations of bullying and harassment based on religion as part of the 2015–2016 Civil Rights Data Collection. This data will help illustrate trends in bullying and harassment based on religion in our nation's schools.

Need to Create an Environment Where All Students, Regardless of Their Faith Background, Are Treated as Persons of Equal Worth Who are Entitled to Mutual Respect: Roundtable Participants stressed that students whose faith is a minority in a particular school, as well as students with no religious affiliation, often are marginalized or misunderstood. Participants emphasized that schools, religious communities, and state and Federal agencies need to be intentional about creating a culture that is respectful of all persons and honors our nation's long commitment to religious diversity and freedom. Other Participants noted that students are reluctant to report bullying and harassment by other students for fear of drawing more attention to themselves.

Addressing the Role that Parents May Play in Contributing to Religious Intolerance in Schools: Roundtable Participants acknowledged that for many students, their views about other religious communities originate from parents at home or from other influences outside of the school building. Participants observed that rather than receiving information about religious pluralism and the need to respect all faith traditions, too often young people see parents and other community members condoning discriminatory actions and behavior.

Addressing the Role the Teachers May Play in Contributing to or Otherwise Perpetuating Student Harassment: While Roundtable Participants recognized the important role that teachers play in supporting diverse and inclusive classroom environments, several Participants expressed concern about some teachers' actions, inaction, or other behavior toward students with respect to harassment based on religion. For example, some Participants stated that teachers who promoted one or more religions as being superior could foster an environment in which harassment of students based on their religion or perceived religion was deemed acceptable. Similarly, some Participants explained that while teachers may not explicitly encourage bullying, they may allow a classroom environment to develop where bullying is viewed as acceptable behavior by not addressing it or challenging stereotypes that are raised towards students of particular religious backgrounds.

Educators' Lack of Awareness or Knowledge About Civil Rights Protections: Despite longstanding protections prohibiting religious discrimination in Title IV and other similar Federal laws, Roundtable Participants commented that many educators do not fully understand how these legal protections translate into specific requirements, practices, and policies in the classroom. As a result, many parents and students are unaware, or not fully aware, of their rights to be educated in an environment free from religion-based discrimination and harassment. Participants also observed that for English Learner students and their families, language barriers often exacerbate this problem. Participants noted that the distribution of Federal guidance, such as "Dear Colleague Letters," to administrators – rather than to everyone in the school community – can serve as a barrier to addressing this issue.

Roadblocks to Teaching Students about Religion in K-12 Classrooms: There was widespread agreement among Roundtable Participants that effectively combating religious discrimination in educational settings will require all students to develop a deeper understanding about, and respect for, different religions and religious practices. Yet Participants recognized that discussions of religion in the classroom raise many difficult issues. When done right, teaching students about religion can increase understanding and reduce bullying and harassment, but inaccurate and stereotypical treatment of certain faiths can lead to greater bullying and harassment. Participants also discussed the need for educators to respect First Amendment concerns. Participants noted related issues, such as how to incorporate teaching students about religion into the curriculum; how to train teachers in this area; the need to encourage parental buy-in and address concerns that teaching students about religion will lead to proselytizing; how to make space for students of minority religions to feel comfortable talking about their faiths if they choose without drafting them unwillingly to speak on behalf of their faith group, as sometimes happens; and the benefits and risks of having guest speakers, such as representatives of religious communities, speaking to students. Some Participants suggested that the most effective approach may involve striking a balance between making education about religion current, accurate, and reflective of diversity within religious traditions without "watering down" the content so much that it offers little instructive and educational value to students. Participants highlighted that there are existing resources that could be useful in this effort.

Access to Reasonable Religious Accommodation: Roundtable Participants stressed the need for ensuring that students have access to reasonable religious accommodations. Participants discussed the importance of individualized accommodations for religious beliefs, such as excusal from school for religious holidays, religious clothing exceptions to school dress codes, and accommodation for prayer during the school day. There was also a recognition that religious accommodations can sometimes raise difficult issues, such as where a particular accommodation may impact the rights of other students, or where accommodations may conflict with curricular goals (e.g., situations where a student may seek to opt-out of a course or part of a course due to religious objections). In light of these and other challenging issues, some Participants opined that additional guidance may be useful.

Challenges Regarding Religious Diversity in Colleges and Universities: Roundtable Participants recognized that there are unique challenges when it comes to addressing issues of religious intolerance in the higher education context. Some Participants noted that while colleges and universities should strive for civil debate on religious and religion-related policy issues, care should be taken not to use the desire for civility to stifle robust debate and minority viewpoints. Somewhat similarly, some Participants expressed concern about student religious organizations not being allowed to choose club leaders using religious criteria. These Participants explained that even where religious student organizations welcome any student to join as a member, it is critical that they have the ability to ensure that leaders of the clubs are members of their particular faith tradition. Others, however, expressed the view that it may not be appropriate to allow a student organization to limit leadership on religious grounds in situations where the organization receives public funding.

Recommendations:

> **Provide Updated Guidance on How Schools Can Teach Students about Religion**: Roundtable Participants recommended that the Federal government provide additional guidance about how educators can incorporate information about religion into the curriculum and classroom discussions in a manner that is accurate, effective, and consistent with constitutional requirements. Participants suggested that substantive instruction for students about the pantheon of religions and religious traditions, in addition to instruction on religious freedom and inclusion, would be very beneficial for students. Participants also highlighted that the Federal government should recognize the need to specifically address such guidance to teachers, not only to administrators. Some Participants suggested that the Federal government consider updating and redistributing the guidance, issued in 1995, by the Federal government on Religion in Public School. (Related guidance was issued by the Department of Education in 2003).

> **Provide Training to Address Bullying and Harassment**: Roundtable Participants noted that specialized training around bullying and harassment is also critical to effectively combating religious discrimination in our schools. Participants noted that both the Federal government and local school districts need to do more to provide parents with tools, resources, and guidance about how to identify signs of bullying at home and how to lead productive discussions with children about whom to report it to, how to respond, and what to do next. Participants also noted that teachers need training to recognize signs of bullying in the classroom, as well as resources to address bullying and harassment that occur through social media or online.

> **Promote Education and Implement Relevant Training**: In addition to receiving education about different religions, Participants uniformly expressed the view that students, teachers, and school administrators should also learn about broader lessons of religious freedom, respect for differences, and inclusivity. One Participant recommended that this could be pursued by explicitly tying religious freedom to civic education and educational programs about the Constitution. Another discussed that an effective tool is to have a student of a particular faith

from a different school come in and talk about his or her experience with religious inclusion. Others suggested various peer mentoring and peer mediation programs. Some Participants recommended that teachers and administrators encourage students to develop student-led initiatives to foster unity and a positive school climate on campus. By engaging on these issues at the front end – as well as by providing students with mediation and conflict resolution training – teachers can ensure that students develop respectful attitudes of other religions to prevent bullying and harassment, and know the response strategies to use when it occurs, Participants said.

➢ **Revise Stopbullying.gov**: Roundtable Participants noted that Stopbullying.gov, a Federal website devoted to providing information about identifying and addressing bullying, is a useful resource but recommended that additional changes be made to improve the effectiveness of the portal. For example, the website contains information about training and guidance, but Participants highlighted that it could be updated to include additional information about resources and programs underway at state and local levels. Along these lines, some Participants also suggested that information contained in the "Resources" section of Stopbullying.gov be improved and streamlined.

➢ **Improve Communication to Ensure All Stakeholders Know Their Rights and are Aware of Existing Resources**: Roundtable Participants stressed the need to make sure community members are aware of existing programs and resources. For example, some Participants suggested that when the Federal government issues guidance documents, such as "Dear Colleague Letters," there should be follow up to gauge whether the guidance is effectively reaching communities at the local level, or whether providing technical assistance to schools may be beneficial. Participants also recommended that the Federal government explore different platforms to communicate information, including the use of social media and video, and find new methods of distributing training and guidance so that it is more likely to reach students, parents, and teachers.

➢ **Increase Training for Relevant Stakeholders**: Rather than simply punishing or criticizing students for holding certain negative stereotypes about different religions, Roundtable Participants suggested that stakeholders, including the Federal government, take steps to better understand the underlying biases that shape those stereotypical views and beliefs. As one Participant commented, "Let's take out the finger-pointing and recognize we all need to work on this." Several Participants thought increased cultural competency training for educators is critical and expressed interest in finding ways for Federal government regional offices to partner with community organizations to develop train-the-trainer programs. Others suggested that mental health professionals need to be involved in these efforts to address the emotional and mental toll that religious-based bullying and harassment has on students.

➢ **Federal Guidance on Title VI of the Civil Rights Act of 1964 and Religion**: Roundtable Participants noted that there still remains confusion about when the prohibition on discrimination based on race, color, or national origin in Title VI of the Civil Rights Act of 1964 (Title VI), which pertains to discrimination in Federally-funded programs or activities, may be implicated in situations where there is religious discrimination that is closely tied to race, color, or national origin. Participants expressed an interest in ensuring that Title VI is consistently enforced across the country in this area. Participants asked for guidance from the Federal government about how Title VI may apply in situations involving religious discrimination in schools.

➢ **Recognize Implicit Bias and Misunderstandings about Religion**: Roundtable Participants mentioned that a lack of understanding, information, and knowledge about diverse religious communities can lead to hurtful, divisive comments and even unintentional discrimination. In addition, Participants observed that there is value in recognizing that we all hold implicit biases, prejudices, and stereotypes, but we can work together to identify these biases, and ensure that we do not act on them or allow such biases to impact our behavior. Participants recommended that the Federal government consider ways to ensure that teachers and others who work in our nation's schools are educated about the role that implicit biases may play in perpetuating religious discrimination.

B. Employment

Title VII of the Civil Rights Act of 1964 (Title VII), which prohibits religious discrimination in employment, is one of the most well-known civil rights protections in our country. Yet, Roundtable Participants highlighted that both employers and employees often lack information about the protections and obligations Federal law provides related to faith-based protections in the workplace. Participants also expressed both concern and frustration regarding the time it takes to resolve claims of religious discrimination. By addressing these issues, collecting more robust data, and leading new outreach efforts, Participants observed that the Federal government has an opportunity to make significant strides in ensuring that all workplaces remain free from unlawful religious discrimination.

Themes, Trends, and Problems:

Discrimination During the Job Application Process: Roundtable Participants expressed concerns that during the pre-employment and job application period, issues related to physical appearance, including religious-related dress, often prevent members of religious communities from receiving a fair and non-biased evaluation. One Participant, citing a common fear of women who wear headscarves and other similar religious coverings, said "the scarf enters the room before I do." Other Participants noted the problem of discrimination faced by individuals with names that are, or are perceived to be, associated with a particular religion, including names perceived to be "Muslim."

Discrimination and Harassment on the Job: Roundtable Participants noted that individuals from less familiar religious communities, particularly those that are – or are perceived to be – Muslim, experience higher levels of religious discrimination and harassment once hired. Other Participants observed that in a number of workplaces it is common for employers to engage in activities, such as all-staff prayers or religious-themed holiday programs, which can lead nonreligious employees and employees of different religions to feel unwelcomed.

Lack of Awareness about Anti-Discrimination Protections: Roundtable Participants reported a lack of awareness by both employers and employees about existing protections under Federal law that prohibit discrimination on the basis of religion in the workplace. Participants noted that some employees – knowing that employers do not allow time for prayer during the workday – choose not to apply for a given job altogether. Employees often do not know about the strict time limits for filing employment discrimination complaints under Title VII and other applicable laws.

Failure to Provide Religious Accommodations: Roundtable Participants expressed concern that many employers do not know about their obligation under Federal law to provide reasonable accommodations based on religion in the workplace, such as accommodating work schedules or dress codes. Participants noted that while most employers train staff on accommodations under other Federal civil rights laws, similar training for religious accommodation under Title VII is frequently absent. Participants also noted that the increase in online job applications, which often automatically screen out applicants who indicate that they are not available certain days without the ability to explain that this is for religious purposes, present a barrier to reasonable accommodation.

Underreporting of Religion-Based Employment Discrimination: Roundtable Participants raised concerns that there is underreporting of religious discrimination in employment settings. As noted above, a number of Participants stated that many employees lack awareness about how to report complaints of religious discrimination. In addition, employees who do suffer and endure discrimination on the job may face pressure – often manifested in implicit and subtle ways – to refrain from complaining or speaking out. Participants commented that employees may fear retaliation from their supervisors and may feel reluctant to cause trouble or raise concerns with their employer.

Length of Time to Resolve Employment Discrimination Charges: Several Roundtable Participants said that the lengthy period of time it often takes the EEOC to resolve charges of discrimination can contribute to a sense of discouragement among those who believe they have suffered religion-based discrimination in the workplace. Participants also noted that the lengthy investigation process leads to confusion about what individuals should do in the meantime. What does the delay mean? Should they return to the job? Should they begin looking for a new job? Participants reported that these types of delays only further perpetuate the concern that the Federal government remains inaccessible as employees look for quick responses when they face employment discrimination.

Culture and Accessibility of Government Agencies: Roundtable Participants described a challenge regarding the accessibility of government, saying that it would be beneficial for their communities to have mechanisms for engaging with complicated Federal agencies and offices. They noted that, particularly in the employment context, the lack of clear information and awareness over what constitutes discrimination serves as a significant barrier to equal and inclusive workplaces.

Recommendations:

> **Improving Education and Awareness for Employees**: Roundtable Participants recommended that the Federal government do more to ensure that the public knows how to meaningfully respond to religion-based workplace discrimination. The need for greater clarity for the public about both employee rights and employer responsibilities was the topic of discussion by multiple Participants. Participants further noted that outreach to employees and employers alike could include providing additional information about deadlines for filing charges of discrimination with the appropriate government agencies, including the EEOC; ensuring that posters in the workplace notifying employees about their rights are more prominently displayed; and connecting with employees through a variety of media platforms, including alternative language newspapers and social media. Some Participants noted that public service announcements may also provide a valuable vehicle and tool to reach employees.

> **Improving Education and Awareness for Employers**: Roundtable Participants stressed that many employers are not fully aware of what they are required to do in order to fully comply with the prohibition against religious discrimination in Title VII. Participants recommended that the Federal government provide targeted efforts and training to employers about their responsibilities. One Participant suggested that the EEOC review instances in which employers have resolved cases through the conciliation process as a mechanism for identifying common employer misconceptions about the law and how other employers could be better informed. Some Participants suggested that the EEOC provide employers with additional materials to ensure that they fully understand their obligation to comply with existing non-discrimination and civil rights laws.

> **Greater Outreach to Impacted Communities**: Roundtable Participants recommended that the Federal government use regional offices and outreach staff to strengthen ties to community

organizations at the local level. Participants identified regional offices of the EEOC as well as U.S. Attorneys' Offices across the country as locations where such points of contact for community outreach could be based. Participants also suggested that Federal agencies have regular lines of communications with faith leaders, including by relying on measures such as periodic meetings or newsletters.

➢ **The Federal Government Should Lead by Example in Religious Accommodations**: When it comes to religious accommodations, Roundtable Participants suggested that the Federal government should lead by example. To highlight this recommendation, some Participants noted the legal disputes with the Federal government about whether observant Sikhs can serve in the U.S. military while showing outward expressions of their faith, such as wearing a turban and growing out a beard. Other Participants noted that the Federal government should make it easier for Federal employees to file religious discrimination charges. Participants highlighted prior Federal guidelines that were issued about religion and the Federal workplace as a useful tool.

➢ **Improve Data Collection**: Participants said greater attention and focus need to be placed on data collection about religious discrimination in employment, and on accurately identifying discrimination against particular faiths as well as against people who identify as nonreligious. While Participants acknowledged that some forms of discrimination – such as refusing to hire an applicant because she wore a headscarf – might be harder to track, they suggested the Federal government prioritize improving data collection while also working with employers and community members to address problems of underreporting.

➢ **Improve Processing Times for Complaints**: Roundtable Participants observed that many individuals who face religious discrimination in the workplace are unwilling to file charges of discrimination with the EEOC in light of the often lengthy investigation process. To that end, Participants recommended that the EEOC expedite its process for reviewing discrimination complaints and provide employees with useful resources so the process is as transparent as possible.

➢ **Autonomy of Religious Institutions**: Roundtable Participants called for greater discussion – both among the public and within Federal agencies – of the principle of autonomy that is reflected in the Title VII statutory exemption, which permits, in specified situations, certain religious organizations to preference the employment of members of their own religion. A number of Participants stressed the need to balance this principle of autonomy with the rights of others against nondiscrimination.

C. Hate Crimes

The fundamental principle that no one should suffer violence simply because of what they believe has led Congress to enact a number of laws that criminalize threats and acts of violence directed towards individuals because of their faith or at houses of worship, including 18 U.S.C. § 247 (Damage to Religious Property) and 18 U.S.C. § 249 (Matthew Shepard and James Byrd, Jr. Hate Crimes Prevention Act of 2009). Unfortunately, too many people in this country continue to suffer harassment and violence because of their faith. Roundtable Participants stressed how Muslim individuals and communities, and those perceived to be Muslim, are facing a backlash of violence and discrimination following recent terrorist attacks in the United States and abroad. Similarly, many highlighted that houses of worship, including mosques and gurdwaras, are seeing an uptick in attacks. Many communities are concerned that they lack the resources and support they need to keep their congregants safe. Several Participants called for the Federal government to enhance its data collection practices, improve outreach to targeted communities, and address some of the root causes of discrimination by facilitating interfaith collaboration and dialogue.

Themes, Trends, and Problems:

Data Collection: Several Roundtable Participants expressed concern, confusion, and frustration over the lack of clear, consistent, and accessible data to track hate crime reporting and prosecutions. For example, Participants cited a wide disparity between the FBI's Uniform Crime Reporting Hate Crime Statistics (in which law enforcement agencies reported 5,479 hate crime incidents involving 6,418 offenses in 2014) and the Bureau of Justice Statistics National Crime Victimization Survey polling-based data (which in 2013 reported an estimated annual average, from 2007 to 2011, of 259,700 nonfatal violent and property hate crime victimizations against persons age 12 or older residing in U.S. households). The disparity among government sources – when combined with different sets of statistics that are regularly reported in the news media – further exacerbates the problem, Participants said. While Participants acknowledged valid reasons for the gap between these numbers, they stated that it would be useful to have greater clarity as to why the numbers differ so significantly. Participants also emphasized that truly accurate data requires a combination of both improved reporting from communities and enhanced training of law enforcement to properly identify and label incidents as hate crimes.

Backlash against Muslims and Individuals Perceived to be Muslim: Roundtable Participants expressed concern that hate violence towards Muslims, as well as individuals who may be perceived to be Muslim, including Sikhs, Hindus, Arabs, Middle Easterners, and South Asians – which has occurred at elevated levels since the terrorist attacks of September 11, 2001 – has only increased in intensity given the terrorist attacks over the past year. One Participant noted that her organization has been tracking these incidents and recorded dozes of threats, violence, and acts of vandalism in the last several months alone. Participants expressed concern in particular about a climate in the media, social media, and society more generally that is contributing to higher levels of bias crimes against these groups.

Underreporting of Religion-Based Hate Crimes: Roundtable Participants repeatedly highlighted that many communities lack information about what constitutes a hate crime under Federal law and generally lack awareness about how to define or report hate-related violent incidents. Participants stated that many individuals not familiar with the intricacies of hate crime laws do not understand the distinction between constitutionally-protected hate speech and criminal activity, as defined by state and Federal statutes. Additionally, language or cultural barriers may hinder effective outreach efforts to some individuals and communities. This is intertwined with concerns regarding underreporting: according to Participants, a lack of awareness can easily lead to individuals failing to register complaints with law enforcement officials.

Violence and Criminal Threats Targeting Places of Worship: Another major area of concern identified by many Roundtable Participants involved an uptick in threats and attacks against houses of worship and religiously-affiliated institutions. When it comes to protecting houses of worship, one Participant who is a pastor explained, often religious leaders and public safety officials may encounter conflicting goals. Religious leaders, on one hand, strive to invite people in – to create an inclusive, welcoming environment. Law enforcement officials, on the other hand, may be inclined to focus on regulating access to specific locations for safety concerns. Moreover, some Participants noted that smaller communities and houses of worship often lack the resources, guidance, and instruction necessary to adequately deal with public safety threats. Many Participants also agreed that often houses of worship do not have established relationships and connections with local law enforcement.

Recommendations:

➤ **Improve Online Information**: To address confusion about hate crime reporting and data collection, what constitutes a hate crime under Federal law, and who to contact in the aftermath of a threat or attack, Roundtable Participants recommended that the Federal government update and revise current online resources in order to make the information more accessible to the public. A number of Participants also suggested that the Federal government consider creating a centralized resource page, similar to Stopbullying.gov, that could include all the relevant information related to combating religion-based hate violence.

➤ **Need for More Robust Data Collection**: Roundtable Participants suggested that Federal law enforcement agencies improve their data collection around hate crime offenses, including information about both victims and perpetrators of hate crimes. Participants observed that this additional information would allow impacted communities and the Federal government to better understand whether there are trends in terms of who is being victimized by hate violence and who is committing hate crimes. Participants noted that this additional data could also be helpful in allowing communities to determine whether there is more they can do to help address systemic causes of hate violence.

➤ **Enhance Awareness about Federal Resources for Protecting Places of Worship**: Roundtable Participants recommended Federal agencies provide additional information about resources available to protect places of worship. Participants recognized that the Federal government already provides an array of resources to help communities protect places of worship; however, they stated that there need to be stronger efforts to promote and share this information. Several Participants suggested that enhanced outreach to religious congregations about when and how to apply for government grants related to safety and security would also be helpful.

➤ **Increase Communication about Prosecutions**: Roundtable Participants recommended that the Department of Justice enhance its communications efforts following hate crime prosecutions, including by more visibly highlighting convictions through press releases and other public announcements.

➢ **Increase Bias Training and Education**: In addition to improving training about hate crimes, a number of Roundtable Participants also suggested that the Federal government do more to address systemic issues around discrimination that may contribute to hate violence. Participants requested that the Federal government lead educational efforts that seek to address bias against religious minorities, including cultural competency and education in constitutional values regarding the free exercise of religion. Some Participants noted that religious organizations can serve as useful partners and allies for the Federal government in these efforts since religious leaders can help teach community members about the values of respect and inclusivity and use interfaith collaboration as a powerful vehicle.

➢ **Strengthening Relationships with Law Enforcement**: To most effectively address and prevent hate violence that targets houses of worship, Roundtable Participants observed that faith leaders need to have direct lines of communication with law enforcement. These Participants noted that beyond calling 911 in the event of an emergency, houses of worship need connections with public safety officials who know their community, recognize the unique challenges they face, and understand the layout of their facilities and the nature of their congregations. The process can simply begin by inviting local law enforcement officials to houses of worship, walking these officials through the facility, and giving them personal knowledge about the community. Participants also suggested that regional Federal agencies, such as U.S. Attorneys' Offices, could be useful in facilitating these relationships.

➢ **Facilitating Interfaith Dialogue and Communication**: Roundtable Participants recommended that the Federal government play a role in helping to facilitate interfaith alliances and similar relationships between diverse religious communities. For example, some Participants noted that U.S. Attorneys' Offices and other regional Federal offices could sponsor interfaith coalitions or host regular community forums where diverse religious leaders have the opportunity to interact and coordinate around combating issues associated with religion-based hate violence. Many Participants noted that the roundtable they attended was one of the first times they had all been in the same room with a diverse cross-section of religious leaders. They observed that, if different religious communities had a way to work together, religious leaders could more effectively send a message that denounces religion-based hate and impact the culture in a positive way. Religion-based hate violence, they explained, could cease to be strictly seen as impacting certain communities, but instead could be opposed by a unified group representing multiple religious affiliations and highlighted as unacceptable conduct. Participants added that religious leaders should explore efforts that lead to greater interaction of people of different faiths, such as "pulpit swaps" and "head/heart/hands" projects, which include learning about a different faith, developing friendships, and working side-by-side on service projects.

D. Religious Land Use

The Religious Land Use and Institutionalized Persons Act of 2000 (RLUIPA) includes provisions protecting individuals, houses of worship, and other religious institutions from discrimination in zoning and land marking laws. Roundtable Participants noted ongoing concerns from municipal officials about the construction of places of worship and observed how houses of worship – particularly those from less familiar religious traditions – often face unlawful barriers in the zoning and building process. Participants, including lawyers who litigate religious land use cases, discussed how many municipalities simply do not know enough about RLUIPA, lacking awareness about both its provisions and how the statute must be interpreted when it conflicts with local or state laws

Themes, Trends, and Problems:

Shifting Tone of Discrimination: Roundtable Participants – including lawyers, advocates, and community members – repeatedly emphasized that while religious congregations continue to face rampant discrimination in the zoning and building processes, the discrimination has become less overt in recent years. As one Participant stated, "the playbook is being re-written." He recalled a conversation with a pastor who said: "They used to come at me and say we don't want more Christians. Now they come at me, and say well, you've got building code issues and traffic [problems]." Religious leaders from other faith backgrounds also highlighted this development. One Participant explained that those opposing the construction of houses of worship have become more organized, more subtle, and more "strategic" in their protests. As another Participant recalled, "People don't come into hearings now and say 'I hate Muslims.' They say, 'the traffic is going to be terrible on [Fridays].'" Some have even distributed literature about how to raise traffic, noise, and congestion concerns. This stems in part, according to some Participants, from previous attempts to use hostile and racist opposition backfiring, leading many municipalities to vote in favor of mosques and Islamic institutions in land use decisions. Despite these changes in tone, Participants stressed that discrimination against houses of worship and religious congregations remains a serious and growing problem.

Municipalities Prioritizing Revenue Collection over Support of Places of Worship: Roundtable Participants pointed out that many municipalities may oppose the construction of houses of worship not out of animus or discrimination, but because they want to attract and incentivize revenue-generating entities, rather than tax-exempt nonprofits. Similarly, one Participant explained, religious land use just simply is not viewed as a critical part of the discussion about zoning and municipal planning. Referencing his communication with municipal officials, the Participant explained, "I've looked at 40 comprehensive plans. Nobody is sitting out there and saying, 'You know what's really important in our community, the religious land use needs.'" However, Participants noted that even in these situations where local leaders do not necessarily harbor animus towards houses of worship, the net result is the same: religious congregations are faced with unfair and unjust land use restrictions.

Lack of Education and Awareness about RLUIPA: Several Roundtable Participants mentioned how municipal officials lack information about RLUIPA, and even those with a passing familiarity with the law view it as a litigation risk rather than a statute protecting fundamental rights. One Participant mentioned that during a recent case RLUIPA was referred to as "an obscure Federal law." Another Participant emphasized that many local officials do not realize that RLUIPA still applies even when it conflicts with their state and local laws. As a Participant commented, "local bureaucrats just want to look at state law. It doesn't even occur to them that there's something out there other than their own ordinances or state law[s]."

Recommendations:

- **Outreach and RLUIPA Education for Local Officials**: Roundtable Participants noted that the Federal government, and particularly the Department of Justice, has an important role to play in helping to educate and inform municipalities about RLUIPA. To that end, some Participants recommended that the Federal government consider distributing details about the statute in a range of accessible and digestible formats; providing best practices and case studies; and when appropriate, sending informational letters to municipalities. Participants also suggested that the Federal government conduct more proactive outreach with organizations and gatherings of municipal attorneys, planning professionals, and insurance carriers, and write articles in trade publications. Getting information about RLUIPA to municipalities before a dispute arises – or early in the process when one does – may help avoid litigation. Participants also noted that the Federal government could help municipalities positively highlight their RLUIPA compliance as part of a broader welcoming campaign toward diverse communities and thus highlight the economic benefits that may accompany compliance.

- **Outreach to Communities**: Roundtable Participants also noted that additional efforts are necessary in order to ensure that religious communities are aware of RLUIPA and the protections the law provides. They suggested that making more literature available and in-person outreach by Justice Department personnel would help this.

- **Address Community Tensions After Zoning Disputes**: Roundtable Participants remarked that following a dispute over a place of worship, communities often need assistance addressing tensions that arise during the complaint, investigation, and litigation processes. Participants observed that the resolution of a legal dispute does not necessarily mean that the underlying systemic issues of discrimination, intolerance, and misunderstanding have been fully addressed. Participants suggested that the Department of Justice's Community Relations Service could be a useful resource in helping to address some of these concerns and improve community relations.

- **Consider Changes to Zoning Codes and Adoption of "Content-Neutral" Standards**: Participants suggested that municipalities may want to consider amending zoning codes to regulate assemblies, rather than places of worship. They noted that this might limit the discrimination and unfair treatment that religious congregations often face in the zoning process. In addition, Roundtable Participants said that the use of "content-neutral standards" by municipalities would be greatly beneficial because such a change would eliminate reliance on terms that may only apply to certain faiths (e.g., "clergy residence") and are not necessarily applicable to all religions.

- **Support Community Partnerships and Interfaith Collaboration**: Roundtable Participants spoke repeatedly about the power of community leaders from different faiths – joining with government officials – to make strong value-driven statements against discrimination. Several Participants noted that while an attorney representing a religious congregation in a given case can make a statement during a press conference, it does not carry nearly the same weight or impact as government officials and community leaders making that statement. Participants emphasized that the Federal government has the ability and responsibility to help lead robust dialogue and facilitate conversations around the values of religious diversity and religious pluralism that led to the enactment of RLUIPA.

III. Conclusion

As documented in this report, communities around the country today – of various faiths, beliefs, and backgrounds – share a series of common concerns. Many feel threatened or discriminated against because of who they are, what they believe, or where they worship. At the same time, we also heard creative solutions and innovate proposals about how to address these challenges. And whether it's preventing and prosecuting religion-based hate crimes on our streets or combating religion-based bullying in our schools, the Justice Department is firmly committed to working closely with our agency partners to lead a wide range of enforcement actions and to develop and implement policy proposals.

But we also know that beyond enforcement solutions and beyond policy proposals, we need dialogue. We need community engagement. And we need places to exchange ideas and share best practices. When we do that – when we take the time to truly talk with, listen to, and learn from one another – we build inclusive, vibrant, and safe communities. And we bring our country closer to the ideals our founders envisioned: a place where diversity is embraced, where respect is celebrated, and where freedom is protected. We look forward to our shared efforts to advance this mission alongside all of you – public officials and community members – in the days and months ahead.

IV. Appendix A: Additional Materials, Contact Information, and Resources

Federal Protections Against Religious Discrimination

Federal law makes it unlawful to discriminate on the basis of religion in many different areas, including those listed below.

- **Housing**: The Fair Housing Act prohibits discrimination in housing because of race or color, religion, sex, national origin, familial status, or disability.

- **Credit**: The Equal Credit Opportunity Act prohibits creditors from discriminating against credit applicants on the basis of race, color, religion, national origin, sex, marital status, age, because an applicant receives income from a public assistance program, or because an applicant has in good faith exercised any right under the Consumer Credit Protection Act.

- **Public Accommodations and Facilities**: Title II of the Civil Rights Act of 1964 prohibits discrimination on the basis of race, color, religion, or national origin in certain places of public accommodations, such as hotels, restaurants, nightclubs, and theaters. Title III of the Civil Rights Act of 1964 prohibits discrimination on the basis of race, color, religion, or national origin in public facilities.

- **Land Use**: The Religious Land Use and Institutionalized Persons Act prohibits local governments from adopting or enforcing land use regulations that discriminate against religious assemblies and institutions or which unjustifiably burden religions exercise. This law also protects the religious exercise of persons who are confined to certain institutions.

- **Education**: Title IV of the Civil Rights Act of 1964 prohibits discrimination on the basis of race, color, sex, national origin, or religion in public schools and institutions of higher learning. Also, Title VI of the Civil Rights Act of 1964 prohibits discrimination on the basis of race, color, or national origin (including actual or perceived shared ancestry or ethnic characteristics) in education programs and activities receiving Federal financial assistance.

- **Federally Assisted Services, Programs, and Activities**: Title VI of the Civil Rights Act of 1964 prohibits discrimination on the basis of race, color, or national origin in federally assisted programs.

- **Employment**: Title VII of the Civil Rights Act of 1964 prohibits employment discrimination on the basis of race, color, sex, religion, and national origin. This law also requires employers to reasonably accommodate the religious beliefs and practices of applicants and employees. Executive Order 11246 prohibits discrimination in employment by federal contractors and subcontractors on the basis of race, color, religion, sex, sexual orientation, gender identity, national origin, disability, or status as a protected veteran.

- **Hate Crimes**: Federal hate crime statutes (18 U.S.C. § 241, 18 U.S.C. § 245, 18 U.S.C. § 249 and 42 U.S.C. § 3631) prohibit violent and intimidating acts motivated by animus based on several bases, including race, ethnicity, national origin, and religious beliefs.

- **Violence against Houses of Worship**: Federal law (18 U.S.C. § 247) criminalizes the use of force or the threat of force to interfere with the exercise of religious beliefs as well as the destruction of religious property, including violent conduct targeting religious houses of worship.

How to Contact the Federal Government

The Federal government is committed to actively enforcing the laws listed above. Individuals who believe that they are a victim of discrimination based on their actual or perceived religion (or any other protected category) should contact the appropriate Federal agency.

Department of Justice – Civil Rights Division
950 Pennsylvania Avenue, N.W.
Washington, D.C. 20530
Phone: (888) 736-5551 or (202) 514-3847
Website: www.justice.gov/crt
Complaint Filing Information: www.justice.gov/crt/how-file-complaint

Department of Education – Office for Civil Rights
400 Maryland Avenue, S.W.
Washington, D.C. 20202-1100
Phone: (800) 421-3481
Fax: (202) 453-6012
Email: ocr@ed.gov
Website: www.ed.gov/ocr
Online Complaint Form: http://www.ed.gov/about/offices/list/ocr/complaintintro.html
(Other Languages)

Department of Homeland Security – Office of Civil Rights and Civil Liberties
Compliance Branch
245 Murray Lane, S.W.
Building 410, Mail Stop #0190
Washington, D.C. 20528
Phone: (866) 644-8360 or (202) 401-1474
Fax: (202) 401-4708
Email: CRCLCompliance@hq.dhs.gov
Website: www.dhs.gov/office-civil-rights-and-civil-liberties
Complaint Forms: www.dhs.gov/file-civil-rights-complaint

Department of Labor – Office of Federal Contract Compliance Programs
Phone: (800) 397-6251
Email: OFCCP-Public@dol.gov
Website: www.dol.gov/ofccp

Equal Employment Opportunity Commission
Phone: (800) 669-4000
The American Sign Language (ASL) Video Phone Line: (844) 234-5122
Email: info@eeoc.gov

Website: www.eeoc.gov
Charge Filing Information: www.eeoc.gov/employees/howtofile.cfm
Field Office Locations: www.eeoc.gov/field/index.cfm

About the Justice Department's Community Relations Service

The Community Relations Service (CRS) is the Justice Department's "peacemaker" for community conflicts and tensions arising from differences of race, color, national origin, gender, gender identity, sexual orientation, religion, and disability. CRS is not an investigatory or prosecutorial agency, and it does not have any law enforcement authority. CRS works with communities to prevent and resolve conflicts based on the actual or perceived religion of community members. By improving communication between religious leaders, universities and schools, elected officials, law enforcement, and community members, CRS supports communities in developing relationships and mechanisms to effectively prevent and respond to conflicts based on religion.

Department of Justice – Community Relations Service
600 E Street, N.W., Suite 6000
Washington, D.C. 20530
Phone: (202) 305-2935
Website: www.justice.gov/crs

About the White House Office of Faith-based and Neighborhood Partnerships

The White House Office of Faith-based and Neighborhood Partnerships builds bridges between the Federal government and nonprofit organizations, both secular and faith-based, to better serve Americans in need. The Office is led by Executive Director and Special Assistant to the President, Melissa Rogers, and can be contacted by emailing WHPartnerships@who.eop.gov. The Office coordinates Centers for Faith-based and Neighborhood Partnerships in various Federal agencies. Each Center forms partnerships with faith-based and neighborhood organizations to advance agency-specific goals.

Center at the U.S. Department of Agriculture
Director: Norah Deluhery
E-mail: collaborate@usda.gov
Website: www.usda.gov/partnerships

Center at the U.S. Department of Justice
Director: Eddie Martin
E-mail: partnerships@usdoj.gov
Website: www.ojp.gov/fbnp

Center at the U.S. Department of Commerce
Director: Aaron Jenkins
Website: www.commerce.gov/office-secretary/center-faith- based-and-neighborhood-partnerships

Center at the U.S. Department of Labor
Director: Teresa Gerton

E-mail: CFBNP@dol.gov
Website: www.dol.gov/cfbnp

Center at the U.S. Department of Education
Director: Rev. Brenda Girton-Mitchell
E-mail: edpartners@ed.gov
Website: www.ed.gov/edpartners

Center at the U.S. Department of Health and Human Services
Director: Acacia Salatti
E-mail: partnerships@hhs.gov
Website: www.hhs.gov/partnerships

Center at the U.S. Department of Homeland Security
Director: Rev. David L. Myers
E-mail: partnerships@fema.dhs.gov
Website: www.dhs.gov/fbci

Center at the U.S. Department of Housing and Urban Development
Director: Paula Lincoln
E-mail: partnerships@hud.gov
Website: www.hud.gov/offices/fbci

Corporation for National and Community Service
Website: www.nationalservice.gov/special-initiatives/communities/faith-based-and-other-community-initiatives-and-neighborhood

Center at the U.S. Agency for International Development
Director: Mark Brinkmoeller
E-mail: fbci@usaid.gov
Website: www.usaid.gov/partnership-opportunities/fbci

Center at the Small Business Administration
Director: Christopher Upperman
E-mail: partnerships@sba.gov
Website: https://www.sba.gov/offices/headquarters/ofbnp

U.S. Department of State Office of Religion and Global Affairs
Special Advisor: Dr. Shaun Casey
E-mail: RGAOffice@state.gov
Website: www.state.gov/s/rga/

U.S. Department of Veterans Affairs
Director: Rev. E. Terri LaVelle
E-mail: vapartnerships@va.gov
Website: http://www1.va.gov/cfbnpartnerships/

Office of External Affairs and Environmental Education at the Environmental Protection Agency
Jerry Lawson and Rosemary Enobakhare
E-mail: partnerships@epa.gov
Website: www.epa.gov

Office of Strategic Partnerships at Peace Corps
Faith Initiative Senior Advisor: Lauren Mamane
E-mail: LMamane@peacecorps.gov
Website: www.peacecorps.gov

Center at the U.S. Agency for International Development
Director: Mark Brinkmoeller
E-mail: fbci@usaid.gov
Website: www.usaid.gov/partnership-opportunities/fbci

The Office also coordinates the President's Advisory Council on Faith-based and Neighborhood Partnerships. This Advisory Council is a group of leaders that makes recommendations on how the federal government can more effectively partner with faith- based and neighborhood organizations.

Government Resources

Department of Homeland Security:

- Posters on Common Muslim American and Sikh American Head Coverings and the Sikh Kirpan

- Background Flyer about the Department's Community Engagement Work

- Language Identification Guide

- Resources to Protect Your House of Worship (FEMA)

Interagency Resources on Bullying Prevention – StopBullying.gov

- An Overview of School Districts' Federal Obligation to Respond to Harassment

- State Anti-Bullying Laws and Policies

- Tip Sheet on Working With Young People Who Bully Others

- Tip Sheet on Misdirections in Bullying Prevention and Intervention

- Training Center: Materials for Community Leaders; Community Action Toolkit; and Misdirections in Bullying Prevention Video

Department of Education:

- [Dear Colleague Letter on Race, Religion, and National Origin Tolerance](#)

- [Dear Colleague Letter on Harassment and Bullying](#) [(Other Languages)](#)

- [Dear Colleague Letter on Religious Discrimination](#)

- [First Amendment Dear Colleague Letter](#)

- [Racial Harassment Investigative Guidance](#)

- [School Climate Surveys](#)

- [Fact Sheet on Harassment and Bullying](#) [(Other Languages)](#)

- [Title IX and Religious Exemptions](#)

Department of Justice:

- [Civil Rights Division Website](#)

- [Webpage with Background Information about Hate Crimes](#)

- [Webpage with Religious Land Use Information](#)

- [Update on the Justice Department's Enforcement of RLUIPA: 2010 – 2016](#)

- [Training Video: Building Relationships with Arab and American Muslims](#)

- [On Common Ground: Law Enforcement Training Video on Sikhism](#)

- [The First Three to Five Seconds: Law Enforcement Training Video on Arab and Muslim Cultural Awareness](#)

- [Resources for Schools: Twenty Plus Things Schools Can Do to Respond to or Prevent Hate Incidents Against Arab-Americans, Muslims, and Sikhs](#)

- [Common Ground Podcast Series](#)

- [Critical Incident Checklist](#)

- [Addressing Community Racial Tension](#)

- [Mediation of Community Racial Disputes and Conflicts](#)

- [Planning for Safe Marches and Demonstrations](#)

Joint Department of Education and Department of Justice Resources:

- Fact Sheet: Combating Discrimination Against Asian American, Native Hawaiian, and Pacific Islander (AANHPI) and Muslim, Arab, Sikh, and South Asian (MASSA) Students (Other Languages)

- Dear Colleague Letter on English Learner Students and Limited English Proficient (LEP) Parents

- English Learners Fact Sheet for LEP Parents (Other Languages)

Equal Employment Opportunity Commission:

- General Background Information on Religious Discrimination

- Facts about Religious Discrimination

- Compliance Manual Section on Religious Discrimination

- Questions and Answers: Religious Discrimination in the Workplace

- What You Should Know About Religious and National Origin Discrimination Against Those Who Are, or Are Perceived to Be, Muslim or Middle Eastern

- For Employees: Questions and Answers on Workplace Rights of Employees Who Are, or Are Perceived to Be, Muslim or Middle Eastern

- For Employers: Questions and Answers on Responsibilities Concerning the Employment of Individuals Who Are, or Are Perceived to Be, Muslim or Middle Eastern

- Fact Sheet on Religious Garb and Grooming in the Workplace: Rights and Responsibilities

- Questions and Answers on Religious Garb and Grooming in the Workplace: Rights and Responsibilities

Department of Labor – OFCCP:

- Executive Order 11246 – Equal Employment Opportunity

- Workplace Rights Fact Sheet

V. Appendix B: Roundtable Participants

Roundtable Location: Newark, New Jersey

Date: March 8, 2016

Topic: Education

Agency Co-Sponsors and Participants: U.S. Attorney's Office for the District of New Jersey; White House Initiative on Asian Americans and Pacific Islanders; Department of Education; Community Relations Service; Civil Rights Division

Community Member Participants: The Roundtable was attended by individuals representing a range of religious and community organizations. Organizations represented include:

Agudath Israel of America
American Civil Liberties Union, New Jersey Chapter
American Federation of Teachers
American Jewish Committee
Anti-Defamation League, New Jersey Region
Bloomfield College
Center for Inquiry
Chhaya Community Development Corporation
Council of Imams of New Jersey
Council on American-Islamic Relations, New Jersey Chapter
General Conference of Seventh-day Adventists
Hindu American Foundation
Human Rights Commission of New York City
Interfaith Alliance
Islamic Society of Basking Ridge
Kahlil Gibran International Academy
Muslim Community Network
National Association of Evangelicals
National Sikh Campaign
New Jersey Association of School Administrators
New Jersey Presidents' Council Executive Board
Passaic County Community College
River Dell Regional School District
Sikh Coalition
South Asian Youth Action
Tannenbaum Center for Interreligious Understanding
Union of Orthodox Jewish Congregations
United Sikhs
Universal Muslim Association of American
World Impact

Roundtable Location: Dallas, Texas

Date: March 29, 2016

Topic: Hate Crimes

Agency Co-Sponsors and Participants: U.S. Attorney's Office for the Northern District of Texas; U.S. Attorney's Office for the District of Kansas; Department of Homeland Security; Federal Bureau of Investigation; Community Relations Service; Civil Rights Division

Community Member Participants: The Roundtable was attended by individuals representing a range of religious and community organizations. Organizations represented include:

> Anti-Defamation League, North Texas/Oklahoma Chapter
> Bridging The Gap Baptist Church (Fort Worth, TX)
> Cathedral of Hope (Dallas, TX)
> Center for Inquiry
> Christian Emergency Network
> Congregation Ohr HaTorah (Dallas, TX)
> Dar El-eman Islamic Center (Arlington, TX)
> Hindu American Foundation
> Interfaith Alliance
> Islamic Association of Tarrant County
> Islamic Society of North America
> Muslim Advocates
> Muslim Public Affairs Council
> North Texas Islamic Council
> Northwood Church (Keller, TX)
> Providence Church (Frisco, TX)
> Rabbinical Association of Greater Dallas
> Southern Poverty Law Center
> Tenth Episcopal District AME Church (Dallas, TX)
> The Potter's House Church (Dallas, TX)
> United Sikhs
> Walnut Hill United Methodist Church (Dallas, TX)
> World Without Hate

Roundtable Location: Birmingham, Alabama

Date: April 20, 2016

Topic: Employment

Agency Co-Sponsors and Participants: U.S. Attorney's Office for the Northern District of Alabama; Department of Labor; Equal Employment Opportunity Commission; Civil Rights Division

Community Member Participants: The Roundtable was attended by individuals representing a range of religious and community organizations. Organizations represented include:

AshaKiran (Huntsville, AL)
Baptist Church of the Covenant (Birmingham, AL)
Becket Fund for Religious Liberty
Birmingham Area Sikh and Muslim Community Leaders
Black Catholic Ministry, Diocese of Birmingham
Center for Inquiry
Council on American-Islamic Relations, Alabama Chapter
First Liberty Institute
Greater Birmingham Ministries, Unity Church of Christianity
Hindu Temple & Cultural Center of Birmingham
Interfaith Alliance
National Association for the Advancement of Colored People, Metro Birmingham Branch
National Sikh Campaign
Samford University
Southern Poverty Law Center
Temple Emanu-El (Birmingham, AL)

Roundtable Location: Detroit, Michigan

Date: May 2, 2016

Topic: Religious Land Use

Agency Co-Sponsors and Participants: U.S. Attorney's Office for the Eastern District of Michigan; Community Relations Service; Civil Rights Division

Community Member Participants: The Roundtable was attended by individuals representing a range of religious and community organizations. Organizations represented include:

> American-Arab Anti-Discrimination Committee
> American Jewish Committee
> Anti-Defamation League, Michigan Chapter
> Becket Fund for Religious Liberty
> Bharatiya Temple of Metropolitan Detroit
> Council on American-Islamic Relations, Michigan Chapter
> Council of Religious Leaders of Metropolitan Chicago
> Dalton & Tomich, PLC
> General Conference of Seventh-day Adventists
> Hindu American Foundation
> Islamic Organization of North America
> Mauck & Baker, LLC
> National Network for Arab American Communities
> Sikh Coalition
> Storzer and Greene
> University of Michigan Detroit Center

Roundtable Location: Stanford, California

Date: May 16, 2016

Topic: Education

Agency Co-Sponsors and Participants: U.S. Attorney's Office for the Northern District of California; U.S. Attorney's Office for the Eastern District of California; U.S. Attorney's Office for the Southern District of California; U.S. Attorney's Office for the Central District of California; U.S. Attorney's Office for the District of Idaho; Department of Education; White House Initiative on Asian Americans and Pacific Islanders; Civil Rights Division

Community Member Participants: The Roundtable was attended by individuals representing a range of religious and community organizations. Organizations represented include:

Afghan Coalition
Alliance Defending Freedom
Anti-Defamation League
Asian Americans Advancing Justice – Asian Law Caucus
Becket Fund for Religious Liberty
California Council of Churches
Church State Council, Pacific Union of Seventh-day Adventists
Communities United Reviving East Africa
Council on American-Islamic Relations, San Francisco Bay Area Chapter
Hindu American Foundation
Interfaith Council of Contra Costa County
Islamic Networks Group
Muslim Advocates
Not in Our Town
Pacific Justice Institute
San Diego State University
San Francisco Board of Education
San Francisco Department on the Status of Women
San Francisco Interfaith Council
San Francisco State University
Sikh American Legal Defense and Education Fund
Sikh Coalition
Silicon Valley Interreligious Council
Stanford Law School, Religious Liberty Clinic
Stanford University
University of California, Berkeley

Roundtable Location: Washington, D.C.

Date: May 26, 2016

Topic: National Issue Review

Agency Co-Sponsors and Participants: Department of Labor; Department of Education; Equal Employment Opportunity Commission; Federal Bureau of Investigation; White House Office of Faith-based and Neighborhood Partnerships; Civil Rights Division

Community Member Participants: The Roundtable was attended by individuals representing a range of religious and community organizations. Organizations represented include:

Agudath Israel of America
American Civil Liberties Union
American Jewish Committee
Anti-Defamation League
Arab American Institute
Becket Fund for Religious Liberty
Center for American Progress
Center for Inquiry
Center for Islam and Religious Freedom
Christian Legal Society
Freedom Forum
General Conference of Seventh-day Adventists
Hindu American Foundation
Interfaith Alliance
Muslim Advocates
Muslim Public Affairs Council
National Sikh Campaign
Religious Action Center of Reform Judaism
Shoulder to Shoulder Campaign
Sikh Coalition
South Asian Americans Leading Together
Union of Orthodox Jewish Congregations
U.S. Conference of Catholic Bishops

Roundtable Location: Washington, D.C.

Date: June 20, 2016

Topic: Defining Religion and Religious Discrimination

Agency Co-Sponsors and Participants: Department of Homeland Security; Department of Labor; Department of Education; Department of Justice; Equal Employment Opportunity Commission

Community Member Participants: The Roundtable was attended by individuals representing a range of religious and community organizations. Organizations represented include:

>American Civil Liberties Union
>American Jewish Committee
>American Muslim Institution
>Becket Fund for Religious Liberty
>Catholic University of America
>Center for Inquiry
>Center for Islam and Religious Freedom
>Christian Legal Society
>Church of Jesus Christ of Latter-day Saints
>Church of Scientology
>General Conference of Seventh-day Adventists
>Hindu American Foundation
>Interfaith Alliance Foundation
>Islamic Society of North America
>Muslim Public Affairs Council
>National Association of Evangelicals
>Native American Rights Fund
>Navigators on Capitol Hill
>People for the American Way Foundation
>Queens Federation of Churches
>Religious Freedom and Business Foundation
>Religious Freedom Center of the Newseum Institute
>Secular Coalition for America
>State Conference of Catholic Bishops
>Union of Orthodox Jewish Congregations
>United Methodist Church General Board of Church and Society

www.ingramcontent.com/pod-product-compliance
Lightning Source LLC
Chambersburg PA
CBHW081538280526
45788CB00010B/3283